MILITARY WARBLER
Plutonia Pentagonus

A
FIELD GUIDE
TO
LITTLE-KNOWN
&
SELDOM-SEEN
BIRDS
OF NORTH AMERICA

By

Ben L. Sill

Cathryn P. Sill

John C. Sill

Illustrations By
John C. Sill

PEACHTREE PUBLISHERS, LTD.

Atlanta

Published by

PEACHTREE PUBLISHERS, LTD.
494 Armour Circle, N.E.
Atlanta, Georgia 30324

Manufactured in the United States of America

Illustrations by John C. Sill
Cover design by Laura Ellis

10   9   8   7

Library of Congress Catalog Card Number 88-61461

ISBN 0-934601-58-5

To the One who has given us real birds
that bring us so much joy

CONTENTS

CONTENTS

EXPLANATION OF FIELD GUIDE

As with all publications of this type, the primary objective is to facilitate ready identification of a particular species in the field. Positive field identification is usually accomplished by a combination of several factors: (1) a general description of the bird, (2) its habitat, song, and range, and (3) final identification by a well respected birder in the group.

While many field guides are available today, none include only new and seldom-seen species. Thus, these other "standard" guides do not represent birding state-of-the-art. Some of the more important characteristics of this field guide are presented in outline form below:

1. As you expect in any quality field guide, this volume is replete with numerous excellent illustrations, detailed descriptions, observation hints, and range maps where appropriate. The name of each species is followed by its scientific (Latin) name.

2. To the best of our knowledge, all species listed here have both male and female individuals. The sex of these birds is marked, where appropriate, near the illustrations. Since not all species have been observed in hand, it is possible that some males are females and vice versa. Birders who ascertain that we have incorrectly marked the sex of a species should keep it to themselves so that we won't have to correct future editions.

Although every attempt has been made to make the Guide readable for both amateur and professional birders, it is unavoidable that the treatment of uncommon species such as these would necessitate the use of technical language on occasion. For example, terms such as "migration," "V-formation," "locally abundant," and "hedgerow" may be used.

A conscious attempt has been made to eliminate ambiguous statements of other field guides. A list of terms often found in other guides compared with the more lucid terminology used here is given on the opposite page.

Remember that the most important thing in field identification is the name of the bird. With the name you can readily look up the bird in a field guide such as this. We hope that you will find this Guide useful in identifying what can sometimes be frustrating and annoying birds.

Terms from Other Guides	Terms Used in This Guide
1. Upper breast	1. Lower neck
2. Slightly smaller than	2. Littler
3. Side of the breast	3. Wingpit
4. Wading bird	4. Bird with non-webbed feet that walks around in shallow water
5. Wingbeats	5. Flapping
6. Flight is swift and direct	6. As the crow flies
7. Beak	7. Bill
8. Bill	8. Beak
9. Ill tempered	9. Fowl behavior
10. Plumage	10. Feathers
11. Soar	11. Fly around in circles without flapping or, muscular aches and pains
12. Chief food is . . .	12. Picky eater
13. Coverts	13. Not used in this guide since we don't know what it means
14. Nocturnal migration	14. Fly by night
15. Feed actively	15. Pig out
16. Flock	16. Whole bunch

ACKNOWLEDGMENTS

A special thanks is due to those individuals who used prepublication copies of this field guide for actual field verifications. Their suggestions and the resulting modifications have produced what we believe is an accurate and easily used reference work. It is, however, high time that those who borrowed these early copies give them back.

LITTLE-KNOWN
&
SELDOM-SEEN
BIRDS

WARBLING CORMORANT
Phoghornum Musicalus

An average-sized, dark bird, the Warbling Cormorant can be safely separated from its close relatives only by its call and its inflatable throat pouch. This species, which is restricted to coastal regions, calls only on foggy days. When calling, its throat pouch is inflated, providing resonance, and its wings are drawn up to either side of its head to reflect the sound. This call is a distinctive kru-ul-ully-ully-argh-hmm-ooah-ah-ahoo-kree-eee-ahwho-mmm-mmm followed by several soft, rather random, lyrical phrases.

OBSERVATION HINT   On foggy days, see above. On sunny days, wait for a foggy day and listen for the call. Once pinpointed, wait for the fog to clear to list the bird.

SPECIALIZED EQUIPMENT   State-of-the-art directional microphone

WARBLING CORMORANT

WARBLING CORMORANT

GILA GULL

Larus Precipitatus

Apparently isolated when the prehistoric seas disappeared, this transient species is locally common only in the southwestern United States. Most recent sightings have occurred in Lower Tornillo Creek, Big Bend, Texas. Little is known of the habits of this secretive bird, since it is typically observed only while feeding in flash-flood areas. While the Gila Gull closely resembles other gulls, it can be identified by the lizard in its mouth and its orange and black legs. Call consists of several loud notes.

OBSERVATION HINT The appearance of this bird is highly erratic and dependent on local weather conditions. When thunderstorm warnings are issued, travel immediately to the nearest gulch or arroyo and erect an observation blind. Be sure to note previous high water marks.

SPECIALIZED EQUIPMENT Life Jacket

GILA GULL

FOUR-TOED SNORKEL BILL
Periscopus Quadridigitatus

An uncommon-to-rare inhabitant of intertidal marshes, this two-foot-long bird spends most of the daylight hours under water, going ashore only at night to dry its feathers. The Snorkel Bill may be tentatively identified by its vertical bill, which moves rapidly, with 2 to 3 inches showing above the water surface. It nests in shallow water on old fish beds with unusually high hatchling mortality rates. Seldom calls. Range varies.

OBSERVATION HINT   Take up a location in a dense spartina tidal marsh on a calm day. Constant surveillance of the marsh fringes may reveal what appears to be a short, erratically moving reed. This is either a Four-Toed Snorkel Bill or a short, erratically moving reed.

FOUR-TOED SNORKEL BILL

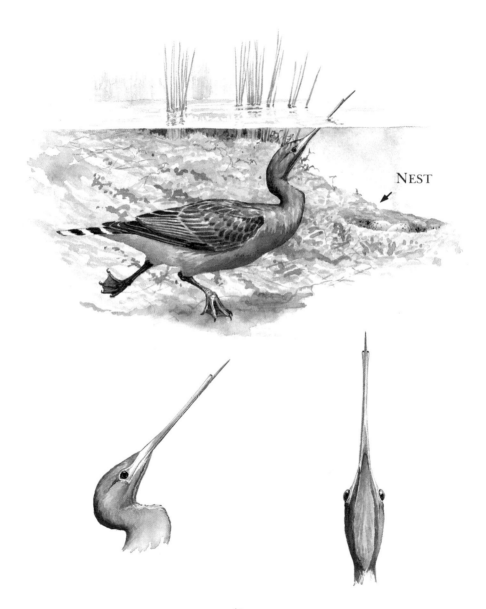

NEST

SOUTHERN SNAKE STRANGLER
Serpentia Constrictus

This rare denizen of southern swamps feeds almost exclusively on water snakes. Classified as a constrictor, this bird squeezes the daylights out of these snakes, causing suffocation. Often two or more birds combine efforts to kill long snakes. This cooperation, rare among birds, is called "team suffocation."

OBSERVATION HINT This bird can be decoyed by placing a rubber snake in an open area of the swamp. When the Snake Strangler finds the snake (which it cannot kill), it will often squeeze for weeks before giving up. During this period, observation is easy.

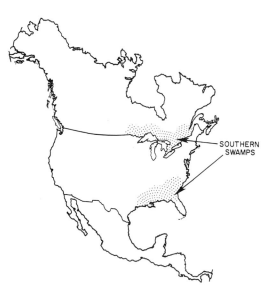

SOUTHERN
SWAMPS

SOUTHERN SNAKE STRANGLER

TEAM SUFFOCATION

MIDDLE YELLOWLEGS
Tringa Intermedius

LEAST YELLOWLEGS
Tringa Minor

Existence of these two new species was substantiated only shortly before this manuscript went to press. Both are similar to the Lesser and Greater Yellowlegs; however, they are readily identified by the fact that the Middle Yellowlegs is smaller than the Greater Yellowlegs and larger than both the Lesser and Least Yellowlegs, while the Least Yellowlegs is smaller than the Greater, Middle, and Lesser Yellowlegs, but is larger than some smaller birds. Many ornithologists believe that a Slightly Lesser Yellowlegs, which is . . . , Oh, nevermind.

OBSERVATION HINT   Yellowlegs flock together.

SPECIALIZED EQUIPMENT   In order to estimate sizes, it is helpful to insert a number of yardsticks in mudflats where Yellowlegs feed.

YELLOWLEGS

GREATEST YELLOWLEGS??

GREATER YELLOWLEGS*

MIDDLE YELLOWLEGS!

SLIGHTLY LESSER YELLOWLEGS?!

LESSER YELLOWLEGS*

LEAST YELLOWLEGS!

VERY LEAST YELLOWLEGS??

11

LONG-RANGE TARGET DUCK
Bombardicus Concentricus

One of the few examples of inverse evolution, the more distinct the markings on this bird, the more likely it is to meet an untimely death. The Atlantic race of this duck normally flew only 20 feet above the ground. Unfortunately, this subspecies has been exterminated, leaving only the midwestern race which flies at 100 feet. Its warning call is a frantic "duck, duck."

OBSERVATION HINT   Once in your sights, this bird is easy to identify. However, for most people, the best chance of getting a good look at a Long-Range Target Duck is a long shot. Use peep sights for the young.

LONG-RANGE TARGET DUCK

OMAHA DABBLER
Order Avies

    The only information about this obviously new species came from a single description supplied by a fisherman in Omaha, Nebraska. He sighted this bird on two different occasions: first, when it was perched in a tree and next, when it was feeding on the lake. Realizing that there was a gap in our data, we sent noted gap biologist John Garton to do some field work on the Dabbler. After an extensive six-day study, his only conclusion was that the males of this species have a slightly larger dotted central portion than do the females.

OBSERVATION HINT   Go fishing.

OMAHA DABBLER

PERCHED

FEEDING

AUGER-BILLED CLAMSUCKER
Screwbeakus Vacuumus

At close range, the spiral grooves on the bill of this rare shore bird are sufficient to provide positive identification. Feeding is accomplished by inserting the bill into the mud until it encounters a clam and then walking in clockwise circles to drill the bill tip through the shell. The clam is sucked out, and the bird rapidly walks counterclockwise to free himself. During feeding frenzies, individuals occasionally begin drilling at such a rate that the entire head will disappear beneath the surface. Birds tend to spiral when flying into a stiff headwind. The Auger-Billed Clamsucker's song, a hearty "chow-der, chow-der" is seldom heard, because in the presence of birders they usually clam up.

OBSERVATION HINT Flocks of the Auger-Billed Clamsucker often follow herds of migrating clams. Best results have been obtained by erecting blinds in the spring along the Atlantic Clamway.

Auger-Billed Clamsucker

SKIA

Sasquatch Yeti

This big footed bird of shores, lakes, and mountains was once widespread in North America, but has now been fragmented into several subspecies. The northeastern, or Nordic race migrates cross-country, while the northwestern, or Alpine subspecies migrates downhill. The southern subspecies is restricted to open water. The Skia is an interesting bird to observe in flight. Concentrations seem to occur in Calgary, Alberta, and in Lake Placid, New York.

OBSERVATION HINT   In winter, Skias are often seen from chair lifts and rope tows.

IDENTIFICATION AID   The various races can be separated by the foot length, although the southern subspecies is difficult to track.

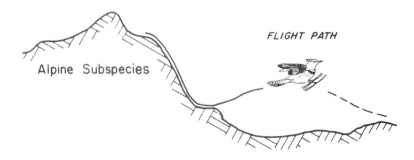

Alpine Subspecies

FLIGHT PATH

SKIA

ALPINE

NORDIC

SOUTHERN
OR WATER SKIA

Elegant Vulture
Regalocorpus Elegans

Except during the short breeding season (May 3 to 5), this bird has the appearance of a Turkey Vulture. The breeding plumage consists of a white neck ruff and a handsome flowing crest. When viewed from below, their soaring habits make it difficult to distinguish them from other vultures. The only close approaches to flying birds have been made with hot air balloons; however, the time required to fill the balloon usually enables the bird to escape. The range of the Elegant Vulture coincides with that of other less elegant North American vultures.

OBSERVATION HINT Between May 3 and 5, place a dead cow in the center of a large, open area, such as a shopping center parking lot. Retire to an upwind blind (or phone booth) and wait.

SPECIALIZED EQUIPMENT Nose clip

ELEGANT VULTURE

VIEW FROM ABOVE

SPRING KITE
Zephyrincus Breezicus

This uncommon-to-rare, rather small bird of prey is easy to identify when detected hovering (in the spring). The bird generally faces into the wind and can remain stationary even against a substantial breeze. Courtship displays include repeated looping with an occasional, sudden crash directly into the ground, possibly explaining the scarcity of this species. Range generally excludes forested areas and electric transmission-line corridors where mortality rates are high.

SPECIALIZED EQUIPMENT

MARCH

S	M	T	W	T	F	S
		1	2	3	4	5
6	7	8	9	10	11	12
13	14	15	16	17	18	19
	NATIONAL	KITE	WEEK			
20	21	22	23	24	25	26
27	28	29	30	31		

SPRING KITE

Night Flying Teeter

Nocturnalis Corpsii

To date, this new species, which represents an entirely new genus, is known only from a single road-killed specimen. Completely nocturnal, this bird has surely evolved to blend in with the night which would explain its overall dark color. It does this so well that the terms "darkness" and "teeter" have become synonymous. Baby, or teeny teeters do not have their full quota of night camouflage and are active only at dusk, when they cannot be seen.

OBSERVATION HINT Routinely, this species is best observed when feeding on lightning bugs. Sometimes, however, these birds will begin feeding during a total solar eclipse, and may be caught afield after the moment of totality is past.

NIGHT FLYING TEETER

SPECIMEN

RINGED GIMPY
Pisa Towerii

   This medium-sized bird is born with one leg shorter than the other. This leg length disparity causes the Ringed Gimpy to walk in circles. The western race of this species is identified by the fact that it walks in larger circles (420 miles) than the eastern race (314 miles). Sexes are most readily determined by the fact that males have a short right leg, whereas females have a short left leg. As a result, males walk clockwise, females counterclockwise; this trait makes breeding opportunities rather unpredictable.

OBSERVATION HINT   Check for recent sightings. Since the flocks travel in circles, observations are cyclic. Stake out the previous location and wait. Based on a walking speed of 0.6 mph, the flock will return every 68 days (91 days for the western subspecies).

SPECIALIZED EQUIPMENT   Newspapers with Gimpy forecasts

RINGED GIMPY

♂

♀

GIMPY RESTING

WADDLEY GROUSE
Obesia Rotundus

This ground-dwelling bird doesn't have much choice. It is difficult to flush since lift from its wings is not sufficient to raise its body more than a few inches above the ground. When not sleeping, the Waddley Grouse spends most of its time eating. Coloration of the bib varies with food and berry stains. Call is a single belch-like note. This highly sought-after bird is essentially self-basting.

OBSERVATION HINT Specimens of this bird can sometimes be found in the frozen food section of gourmet shops. Such sightings can only be added to your grocery list, however.

WADDLEY GROUSE

PIGGING OUT

FULL FLIGHT

SERVING SUGGESTION

BLUNT-BILLED WOODPECKER
Petripeckus Horizontalis

Rare and local, primarily due to lack of habitat renewal. The last remaining population of this medium-sized ladder-backed woodpecker is limited to a small area in the southwestern desert where it receives complete protection. Fallen trees usually serve as nesting sites. Flight is distinctive, often appearing as if the bird is spatially disoriented. Call is a series of short moans. Feeds primarily on silica borers; note the eye color changes from its customary white appearance to red while the bird is actively feeding.

OBSERVATION HINT   Found only in the petrified forest region of Arizona.

BLUNT-BILLED WOODPECKER

ADULT
8:00 AM

JUVENILE

5:00 PM

GREAT-TOED CLAPBOARD PECKER
Magnificent Digitus

This member of the woodpecker family has the obnoxious habit of searching for food on the exterior of residential homes. One subsidiary subspecies is found only in substantially suburban subdivisions, using its great toe to hang from gutters. In the Southwest, this species has apparently hybridized with the Blunt-Billed Woodpecker and is attacking adobe homes. Feeding activity peaks about an hour before the alarm clock rings.

OBSERVATION HINT   Go to an area frequented by the Clapboard Pecker. Build a house.

SPECIALIZED EQUIPMENT   Lumber, hammer, nails

GREAT-TOED CLAPBOARD PECKER

WHITE-LINED ROADRUNNER

Geococcyx Alba-linearis

(FORMERLY MACADAM ROADRUNNER)

Believed to have evolved as a separate species only in recent years, this fairly large terrestrial bird is rapidly extending its range. Although widespread, its numbers remain low from high mortality. It runs quite rapidly (up to 35 mph), but this, unfortunately, is below the minimum allowable speed in its habitat. At present, the populations are restricted to principal federal transportation corridors; however, a few stray birds have been seen on state and county lands. Feet have a unique radial tread pattern. Environmental noise can obscure the call, which is an occasional Beep.

OBSERVATION HINT   Can at times be seen from rest areas and exit ramps.

SPECIALIZED EQUIPMENT   Radar gun

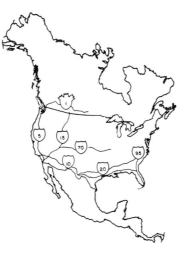

WHITE-LINED ROADRUNNER

DEFENSE POSTURE

GIANT-BILLED SNAPPER
Oralus Giganteus

This fairly common bird with sedentary habits is seldom seen. It spends most daylight hours with its bill resting in the crotch of a tree. It uses its tongue, which appears as a small worm, to entice Worm-Eating Warblers into its open mouth. The Snapper is highly territorial, with the typical territory measuring approximately 6 inches by 6 inches.

OBSERVATION HINT Since this species is a night migrant, it can sometimes be seen in car headlights, dragging its beak along the shoulders of remote roads.

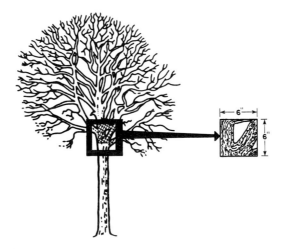

GIANT-BILLED SNAPPER

TONGUE DETAIL

SPOON-BILLED HUMMINGBIRD
Debilliz Compressed

At a glance, this average-sized hummingbird is easily confused with the more common Fork-billed Hummingbird. This species is totally insectiverous, its flattened bill enabling it to catch insects attracted to flowers. The aerial courtship display of the male involves rapid flight in an indented oval, commonly called "spooning."

OBSERVATION HINT Since positive identification cannot be made with a profile view of the bird, best views are obtained if two observers work an area together, moving so as to remain at right angles to each other.

AID IN IDENTIFICATION Whereas the Fork-billed Hummingbird moves its wings at a rate of 58 beats per second, the Spoon-billed Hummingbird has a wing-beat of 62 beats per second. It helps to count by two's.

SPOONING FLIGHT

SPOON-BILLED HUMMINGBIRD

♂

♀

LEAST MINITWIT
Awfulii Smallus, Jr.

This smallest of all functioning birds has always
been a problem taxonomically since it is so itsy bitsy.
Swarms of the Least Minitwit are often seen in barn-
yards, associating as they are known to do with flies.
They have evolved protective mimicry, and have been
known to gather around garbage, walk on ceilings, and
buzz in bedrooms after the lights are out. Their call is a
soft hmmmmm.

OBSERVATION HINT Since a magnifying glass is
almost essential to differentiate this species from flying
insects, sampling is required. Best results have been
obtained by covering a fly swatter with foam rubber,
since squished birds cannot be legitimately added to a
life list.

LEAST MINITWIT

LIFE SIZE

AMERICAN BUNTING

Patrioticus Americana

A common bird in Colonial times, the American Bunting is now rarely seen. Its previous abundance was such that many colonial leaders supported this species as our national bird. In the early 1900s, the American Bunting population was decimated by milliners for Independence Day Parade hats. Following the bicentennial festivities of 1976, the population has increased, and indications are that it is reclaiming some of its original habitat from the English Sparrow. There are now stable colonies in the Philadelphia, Boston, and Washington, D.C. areas.

OBSERVATION HINT Construct a blind on an Independence Day Parade route in one of the above three cities. Drape it with Union Jacks, and wait for the action to start.

SONGOGRAM —

AMERICAN BUNTING

EASTERN SPIDER SPITTER
Salivatus Ptuii

Named for its feeding habits, this species spits small, spherical, sticky, stinging spit salvos at sprightly, speckled spiders, slightly smaller sizewise than weevils, worms, warts, and wolves. Often Spider Spitters splatter spewed spent spit, spreading spongy spray spots all over the place. Call is a muffled "sp . . . sp . . . sp. . . sp."

OBSERVATION HINT Spider Spitters spend spring saving saliva, so search swamps and springs.

SPECIALIZED EQUIPMENT Binocular lens cleaning fluid

EASTERN SPIDER SPITTER

SMALL FLYCATCHER
Empidonax Smallii

This small bird is another in the genus *Empidonax* and is particularly difficult to identify, since it has no field marks. The best approach is to look at the wings, tail, and feet. However, other parts of the bird can also be looked at, if you like. It is so similar to other species in this genera that even individual birds have difficulty with identification. This drastically reduces mating opportunities and apparently accounts for its small population. A further complicating factor is that males and females are unsure of their own sex, thus compounding problems. The call of this species is do-fa-do-re-la-la-me-so-ti-ti-do, although it is known to mimic other flycatchers.

OBSERVATION HINT   Most often seen when birding alone.

SMALL FLYCATCHER

SMALL FLY

CATCHER

GILDED WORM WEAVER
Loomus Caterpillarii

A species distantly related to both the vireos and warblers, it is most easily identified during the nesting season. This colorful bird constructs its nest of live worms and lines it with wooly caterpillars. Since a great deal of time is devoted to nest repair, little time is spent in incubating the eggs and few breeding successes have been reported. Studies show that a typical nest comprises: 7% Bag Worms, 33% Wooly Caterpillars, 22% Tent Caterpillars, and 38% Wiggle Worms.

GILDED WORM WEAVER

MILITARY WARBLER
Plutonia Pentagonus

This small, elusive warbler is difficult to find, since it feeds in dense thickets. Apparently evolving as a mutant from early nuclear tests, this bird is now common only on widely-scattered, high-security military bases. Call is a bugled "you can't get 'em up, you can't get 'em up, you can't get 'em up in the morning." The tail pattern indicates some sort of social rank.

OBSERVATION HINT Since access to high-security installations is not possible, it is necessary to sneak onto the base. In addition, the Military Warbler is so well camouflaged that it cannot readily be seen. This fact is sufficient proof to list the bird. The young may sometimes be attracted with C-rations.

SPECIALIZED TRAINING Must be able to do the 50-yard belly crawl in less than 40 seconds.

MILITARY WARBLER

FLEDGLING　　　　FIRST YEAR　　　　CAREER

Monarch Warbler
Insectus P. Similaris

This brightly colored bird has escaped detection for many years because of its peculiar habit of migrating with large flocks of Monarch Butterflies. While heavier bodied than the Monarchs, the wing pattern of this species is a surprising match to those of the butterfly. Predators apparently see this bird as a butterfly with a weight problem.

OBSERVATION HINT This species can best be observed at close range by examining the front grill of your vehicle after driving through a flock of Monarch Butterflies. Remember to drive slowly, since only live specimens can be added to your life list.

SPECIALIZED EQUIPMENT Car with fine mesh grill

MONARCH WARBLER

EGG

53

TEXAS WARBLER
Dendroica Texanus

The largest member of the genus *Dendroica,* this species is difficult to identify since it is the most rapid flier. It is also the most beautiful, has the loudest song, is the most ferocious, and molts most rapidly. A highly aggressive species, it feeds on tarantulas, bats, and small snakes. Song is often likened to the first few bars of "The Yellow Rose of Texas."

OBSERVATION HINT   This species must be viewed flying left to right for the diagnostic eye patch to have the shape shown. For birds flying in the other direction it is necessary to view them in a mirror (to reverse the image).

SPECIALIZED EQUIPMENT   Wide angle mirror

Texas Warbler

CHOWING DOWN

SPLIT-WINGED SWIFT
Quadriflappus Fleetum

This smallish swift is most often identified by its fast, erratic flight, cigar-shaped body, and its "four wings." The unique wing structure of this species is seldom observed because of its flight habits, but can be seen with high-speed aerotelephotovideography, or with the bird in hand. This "four wing" adaptation likely occurred so that the bird could perform foolish stunts during courtship. Early French Canadian observers nicknamed this bird "Petit Aerodeux" (Little Biplane). Recent studies have shown that molting order in the Split-Winged Swift is upper left, lower right, lower left, upper right. When not on the wings, this bird spends most of its time preening. Not known for its song.

SPECIALIZED EQUIPMENT   Aerotelephotovideograph film and quadripod mount

COURTSHIP FLIGHT

SPLIT-WINGED SWIFT

STUNT FLYING

GREATER WANDERING VAGRANT
Casualus Wandererii

Upon arrival in the spring, this species wanders in a seemingly erratic pattern over much of North America before returning somewhere south in the fall. Most sightings are made when this bird is either coming or going. To date nesting grounds have not been located, and some information indicates that it may carry its nest along on its travels. It is not yet clear how first-year young are imprinted so that they can wander properly. Song is mmm-eeet-mi-n-ss-aint-lu-ee-lu-ee, repeated several times.

OBSERVATION HINT   Finding this bird in the field is truly a hit and miss proposition. Best observations are made by looking at the illustration on the facing page.

GREATER WANDERING VAGRANT

EN ROUTE?

PRAIRIE MOLTER
Corpus Unkemptus

The range of this cardinal-sized bird is limited to the few remaining tall grass prairies in the United States and Canada. Unlike other birds which molt at prescribed times, the Prairie Molter molts continously, exposing the bird's down. As a result, these birds generally look disheveled and may have different appearances depending on which portion of their little bodies is molting. Early settlers were terrified of this bird, fearing that it carried an incurable avian mange. In flight, it may be identified by the trailing stream of dislodged feathers. Pairs can be quite handsome since the down of the male is blue, and that of the female is red. Young birds are a uniform brown color that serves as camouflage by simulating buffalo chips. With the decline of the buffalo, this resemblance made them easy prey. The eggs also molt.

OBSERVATION HINT   Drive 3.2 miles south on Highway 211, turn right and continue for 1.5 miles on County Road SR763. Immediately past a small unnamed stream, stop at a large pasture on the right. Check the eighth fence post. A Prairie Molter was seen here last year.

SPECIALIZED EQUIPMENT   This book.

PRAIRIE MOLTER

EASTERN NARROW SPARROW
Endomorphus Unbelieveably Thinus

In profile, this bird appears as a typical Savannah Sparrow. However, the body of this species is laterally compressed, being less than an inch thick. This species travels in flocks, and frequents cut-over cornfields. When alarmed, all individuals turn to face the intruder and freeze, thus appearing as a field of stubble. Call is a single thin whistle.

OBSERVATION HINT   Contact the owners of any field where this species is believed to feed and obtain permission to flush the birds. Since the Eastern Narrow Sparrow will maintain its frozen posture for indefinite periods, the most successful means of flushing this species is to set the field on fire. Best observations are made from upwind.

SPECIALIZED EQUIPMENT   Fire extinguisher

EASTERN NARROW SPARROW

DEFENSE POSTURE

LESSER SHEDDING SPARROW
Spizella Nudus

This bird was long considered a subspecies of the field sparrow; however, recent study has shown that it is indeed a separate species. Conclusive identification is quite difficult except during the molting season (first full moon following the second Thursday after the vernal equinox, providing all chance of frost is past). The Shedding Sparrow doesn't actually molt, but sheds the entire skin, apparently a holdover from its reptilian ancestors. If flushed immediately after shedding, it is easily recognized by its bright pink color and rapid gait. Often sings exposed on a perch.

OBSERVATION HINT Erect a blind in fields identified by the presence of shed skins and wait for the birds to return, generally on foot. If this doesn't get results, try using Rock Cornish Game Hens as decoys.

LESSER SHEDDING SPARROW

BIBLIOGRAPHY

1. *Myopic Birders Guide — Near Sightings of Rare Birds,* by C. N. Outhing.

2. *Field Guide to Guano,* by Fir T. Lizer.

3. *Trinoculars for Better Birding,* by I. C. DeBirdie.

4. *Trapping Birds with Household Items,* by Tye M. Down.

5. *Attracting Vagrants, Exotics, and Accidentals to Your Feeder,* by I. Markham.

6. *101 Things to Do with Last Year's Bird Nests,* by Fern O. Reason.

7. *A Fleeting Glimpse,* by Ima Lister.

8. *Bird Banding with Tire Weights,* by Day R. Grounded.

9. *Communal Molting,* by Arnt U. Cold.

10. *What's All the Flap About: A New Look at Bird Migration,* by I. Ben South.

11. *Bird Songs for the Shower,* volume 1: "Dipper, Scrub Jay, Water Pipit," by Bubba Bath.

12. *Spelunkers Guide to Birding: A New Perspective,* N. D. Dark.

13. *Pelagic Birds of Nebraska,* by Furd Burfle, PhD.

SOURCE OF NEW BIRD SPECIES

For many years following the turn of the century, no new bird species were found in North America. As a result, it is natural to ask why, in recent years, a sufficient number of new species have been found to merit a new field guide. To help unravel this mystery, some of the best bird brains in North America have been consulted for their theories. Some individuals have offered outlandish ideas; however, one theory received repeated support. We believe this theory to be reasonable, and briefly describe the justification for it below.

Figure 1 gives a history of the number of new North American bird species identified every five years beginning in 1950. It is obvious that starting in 1965, substantial numbers of new species were being reported. To help determine the reason for this, additional charts have been constructed utilizing various candidate phenomena.

After an exhausting search, the most likely causes have been summarized in Figures 2 through 7. Careful scrutiny of these data indicate a strong correlation between UFO sightings (Figure 6) and the number of new species reported (Figure 1). Could it be then that most of the new birds being seen have been placed here by aliens, possibly as an experiment of some kind? How are we to know?

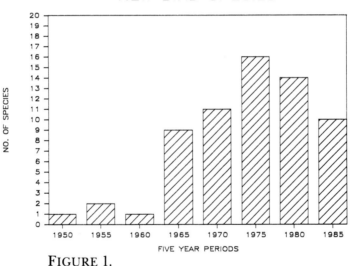

FIGURE 1.

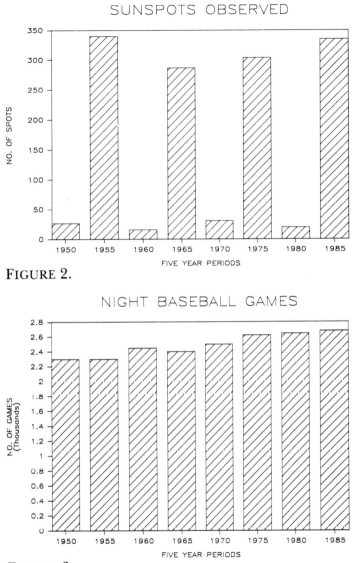

FIGURE 2.

FIGURE 3.

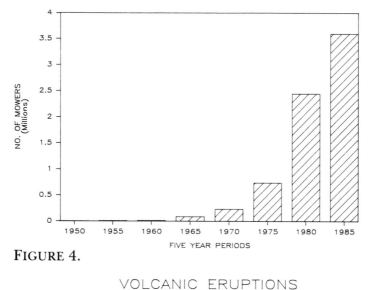

FIGURE 4.

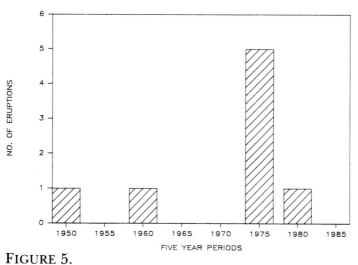

FIGURE 5.

UFO SIGHTING RECORD

FIGURE 6.

NATIONAL DEBT

FIGURE 7.

73

FIELD NOTES

DATE _____

WEATHER CONDITIONS _____

BIRD INFORMATION   Circle the correct answers

Color	dark	light	colorful		
Size	small	medium	large		
Flying Speed	pokey	OK	Wow!		
Wings	1	2	more		
Habitat	air	water	twig		
Legs	short	long	thin	wrinkled	
Flight Direction	N	S	E	W	other
Weight	slim	chunky			
Waist (inches)	1 2 4 6 8 10	fat			
Location	here	there	everywhere		

Observer Competency   a.   Recognizes binoculars
                        b.   Knows someone with binoculars
                        c.   Owns binoculars

SKETCH   Include a head, body, tail, and feet on the end of the legs.

FIELD NOTES

DATE _____

WEATHER CONDITIONS _____

BIRD INFORMATION   Circle the correct answers

Color	dark	light	colorful	
Size	small	medium	large	
Flying Speed	pokey	OK	Wow!	
Wings	1	2	more	
Habitat	air	water	twig	
Legs	short	long	thin	wrinkled
Flight Direction	N	S	E	W	other
Weight	slim	chunky		
Waist (inches)	1 2 4 6	8 10	fat	
Location	here	there	everywhere	

Observer Competency   a. Recognizes binoculars
                                       b. Knows someone with binoculars
                                       c. Owns binoculars

SKETCH   Include a head, body, tail, and feet on the end of the legs.

FIELD NOTES

DATE _____

WEATHER CONDITIONS _____

BIRD INFORMATION   Circle the correct answers
_____

Color	dark	light	colorful		
Size	small	medium	large		
Flying Speed	pokey	OK	Wow!		
Wings	1	2	more		
Habitat	air	water	twig		
Legs	short	long	thin	wrinkled	
Flight Direction	N	S	E	W	other
Weight	slim	chunky			
Waist (inches)	1 2 4 6	8 10	fat		
Location	here	there	everywhere		

Observer Competency   a. Recognizes binoculars
                        b. Knows someone with binoculars
                        c. Owns binoculars
_____

SKETCH   Include a head, body, tail, and feet on the end of the legs.

FIELD NOTES

DATE _____

WEATHER CONDITIONS _____

BIRD INFORMATION   Circle the correct answers

Color	dark	light	colorful	
Size	small	medium	large	
Flying Speed	pokey	OK	Wow!	
Wings	1	2	more	
Habitat	air	water	twig	
Legs	short	long	thin	wrinkled
Flight Direction	N	S	E	W	other
Weight	slim	chunky		
Waist (inches)	1 2 4 6	8 10	fat	
Location	here	there	everywhere	

Observer Competency   a.   Recognizes binoculars
b.   Knows someone with binoculars
c.   Owns binoculars

SKETCH   Include a head, body, tail, and feet on the end of the legs.

FIELD NOTES

DATE _____

WEATHER CONDITIONS _____

BIRD INFORMATION   Circle the correct answers

Color	dark	light	colorful		
Size	small	medium	large		
Flying Speed	pokey	OK	Wow!		
Wings	1	2	more		
Habitat	air	water	twig		
Legs	short	long	thin	wrinkled	
Flight Direction	N	S	E	W	other
Weight	slim	chunky			
Waist (inches)	1 2 4 6	8 10	fat		
Location	here	there	everywhere		

Observer Competency   a. Recognizes binoculars
b. Knows someone with binoculars
c. Owns binoculars

SKETCH   Include a head, body, tail, and feet on the end of the legs.

FIELD NOTES

DATE _____

WEATHER CONDITIONS _____

BIRD INFORMATION   Circle the correct answers
_____

Color	dark	light	colorful		
Size	small	medium	large		
Flying Speed	pokey	OK	Wow!		
Wings	1	2	more		
Habitat	air	water	twig		
Legs	short	long	thin	wrinkled	
Flight Direction	N	S	E	W	other
Weight	slim	chunky			
Waist (inches)	1 2 4 6 8 10	fat			
Location	here	there	everywhere		

Observer Competency   a. Recognizes binoculars
                        b. Knows someone with binoculars
                        c. Owns binoculars
_____

SKETCH   Include a head, body, tail, and feet on the end of the legs.

FIELD NOTES

DATE _____

WEATHER CONDITIONS _____

BIRD INFORMATION   Circle the correct answers

Color	dark	light	colorful		
Size	small	medium	large		
Flying Speed	pokey	OK	Wow!		
Wings	1	2	more		
Habitat	air	water	twig		
Legs	short	long	thin	wrinkled	
Flight Direction	N	S	E	W	other
Weight	slim	chunky			
Waist (inches)	1 2 4 6 8 10	fat			
Location	here	there	everywhere		

Observer Competency   a.   Recognizes binoculars
b.   Knows someone with binoculars
c.   Owns binoculars

SKETCH   Include a head, body, tail, and feet on the end of the legs.

ABOUT THE AUTHORS AND ILLUSTRATOR

John Sill is a prize-winning and widely published wildlife artist who illustrated ABOUT MAMMALS and ABOUT BIRDS, and both illustrated and co-authored A FIELD GUIDE TO LITTLE- KNOWN AND SELDOM- SEEN BIRDS OF NORTH AMERICA, as well as ANOTHER FIELD GUIDE TO LITTLE-KNOWN AND SELDOM-SEEN BIRDS OF NORTH AMERICA and BEYOND BIRDWATCHING. A native of North Carolina, he holds a B.S. in wildlife biology from North Carolina State University.

Cathryn Sill is an elementary-school teacher in Franklin, North Carolina, and the author of ABOUT MAMMALS and ABOUT BIRDS. With her husband John and brother-in law Ben Sill, she co-authored the FIELD GUIDES and BEYOND BIRDWATCHING.

Ben Sill, John Sill's brother, co-authored the FIELD GUIDES and BEYOND BIRDWATCHING. He lives with his wife and two daughters in Clemson, South Carolina, where he is a professor of civil engineering at Clemson University.